Hello Max:

Happy Birthday! Hope you enjoy this look, from the English countryside.

Love,
Uncle Mike

STORIES OF BENJAMIN

By T. Barrie Simmons
Illustrations by
Trudy Friend

Book I

SPELLBOUND BOOKS

Published by Spellbound Books
162 Bush Road, Cuxton, Kent ME2 1HB

Copyright © T. Barrie Simmons 1987

ISBN 1-870748-00-X

Designed by T. Barrie Simmons
Set in 12pt Century by Style Photosetting, Tunbridge Wells
Printed by Errey's Printers Group, Heathfield, England
Bound by Acfords, Chichester, Sussex
Logo-Calligraphy: Jenny & David Hunter,
100 Ravenscroft Road, Beckenham, Kent

Illustrations
by
Trudy Friend

CONTENTS

The Mouse House   7

The Picnic 17

Benjamin's Kite 29

Benjamin's Birthday 39

Benjamin's Castle 49

The Happy Dream 61

The Little Tree 75

With love
for my children.

. . . *sent Benjamin out to play with a small wire loop to blow bubbles.*

The Mouse House

Benjamin Mouse was a very ordinary mouse. He was also a very small mouse and this was very troublesome to him because he had two sisters, both of them quite a bit bigger than Benji (as his mother called him to his annoyance).

He played by himself most of the time, and tried to help his mother when he could — and this was one of his problems — because his mother always seemed to be busy.

One day Benjamin was watching his mother doing the washing and he asked her why she put white powder in the wash. "To make the clothes clean of course," she said. 'Why don't you use soap?" asked Benjamin (he was always asking questions you see, which often annoyed his mother).

"Because soap takes too much time and besides washing powder makes more bubbles, see," and she scooped out some of the warm, frothy water in a cup, and sent Benjamin out to play with a small wire loop to blow bubbles.

Maybe if I put washing powder in the bath I will save lots of time.

Before very long he heard his mother calling him. "Benji, come along in — hurry up now, you know I'm busy." "Just look at you," his mother scolded, "How did you get so dirty blowing bubbles, now I shall have to give you a bath. If only I had more hours in the day."

Benjamin thought about this; then he had an idea.

"Why don't I help make a really quick clean bath. Maybe if I put washing powder in the bath I will save lots of time. That will make Mummy really pleased." So that is what he did.

"Go and call your sisters while your bath is running," said his mother. So Benjamin went outside and called his sisters, but there was no answer.

After a long search Benjamin finally had to admit defeat.

Forgetting the running bath water he went past the garden shed, and through the back gate to look for his sisters. Unknown to him they had heard him calling and hidden behind the garden shed. After a long search Benjamin finally had to admit defeat. So reluctantly he returned home, upset that he hadn't found his sisters but sure that he had done his best (as he always tried to do, even if he was a little forgetful).

When Benjamin walked in through the back gate he heard a commotion in the house, and when he opened the back door he saw there was definitely a big commotion.

There were his mother and his sisters, surrounded by a mountain of frothy white foam.

There were his mother and his sisters, surrounded by a mountain of frothy white foam. " And just where do you think you've been Benjamin?" said his mother in a very cross voice.

He knew he was in deep trouble, because his mother only called him by his proper name when she was really angry with him. "I've been looking for my sisters," he said in rather a weak voice. "Well they came in straight away like good little mice," said his mother. "Why do you always have to be so naughty and go wandering off?"

Benjamin tried to explain but the look on his sisters' faces stopped him. "Whatever made you put all my washing powder in your bath?" his mother continued. "I was only trying to save you time," said Benjamin tearfully, "You said that washing powder was much quicker than soap so I thought I would help you."

Little Benjamin could see that he had caused a lot of trouble and he tried very hard not to cry.

. . . his sisters had hidden from him.

"I don't know what your father is going to say when he comes home?" said Mrs Mouse. At this point Benjamin's two big sisters decided to take pity on him, so while Benajmin's mother washed him in the big kitchen sink (which was not nearly so much fun as a bath), his sisters cleaned up the foamy mess.

When Benjamin's father came home the house was really clean and shiny — most of it having been covered in foam — and he asked Benjamin and his two sisters if they had been good little mice.

Benjamin's mother said he ought to tell his father what he had done, so he did, and Mr Mouse laughed and laughed when he heard about the house full of foam. But Benjamin never said what he suspected — that his sisters had hidden from him, behind the garden shed.

. . . he tripped over the broom.

The Picnic

The sun that shone on Benjamin was so hot, it reminded him of baking day when his mother opened the oven door. The air was so still he couldn't fly his kite or even sail his boat on the garden pond.

His sisters had gone to pick apples to make an apple crumble — one of Benjamin's favourites — but he was so hot even the walk to the orchard was too much for his little legs.

So Benjamin walked indoors where it seemed so dark he could hardly see at all. Unfortunately Benjamin walked in just as his mother was sweeping the kitchen floor and he tripped right over the broom. "Why aren't you out in the nice sunshine?" said his mother, picking him up. "It's too hot, and I don't know what to do," he replied, as his mother rubbed his leg.

...*"kitchen chairs and a tablecloth and then you can make a tent."*

"Well, we can't have you getting under my feet, take this broom outside and I'll bring two kitchen chairs and an old tablecloth and then you can make a tent."

Benjamin thought this was a really good idea. Very soon he was really enjoying himself. His sisters came back with a big basket of apples and they wanted to play in his tent. Of course, it wasn't quite big enough for all three of them.

This problem was soon overcome by bringing out the rest of the kitchen chairs together with all the tablecloths, cushions, rugs and a little table.

By this time they were very thirsty and not a little hungry as well, so the sisters went into the kitchen and soon came back with glasses, lemonade and home-made shortcake.

. . . their father found them as he trundled the lawn mower out to cut the lawn.

After all this preparation and tent building, eating shortcake and drinking lemonade, the three little mice were quite tired. So tired in fact that they were fast asleep when their father found them as he trundled the lawn mower out to cut the lawn.

Father mouse looked at all the things his children had taken to make their tent, then at the three sleeping mice, and lastly at the lawnmower, then he made a decision. It was much too hot to move all the chairs and start mowing the lawn, so he quietly put the mower back into the garden shed. Then he brought out his deckchair and a book. Very soon he was asleep.

. . . father mouse asleep with a book over his nose.

Mother mouse had finished her housework and was sitting in her armchair sewing — she had decided it was much too hot to go outside — and she liked to sew when everyone was out of the house, so she could have some "peace and quiet."

Presently she got up and went into the kitchen to make some tea. This was to make Mother mouse very angry. All the cupboards and drawers in the kitchen were open. All the chairs were missing, indeed the kitchen really was in quite a mess!

She walked out into the back garden and saw Father mouse asleep with a book over his nose. Then she saw where all the things from the kitchen had gone. They had been made into a tent — with Benjamin and his two sisters somewhere inside — asleep.

. . . upset the deckchair (which collapsed) and he fell
in an untidy heap on top of it.

"What's the meaning of all this?" she cried, at which Father mouse jumped, upset the deckchair (which collapsed) and he fell into an untidy heap on top of it.

Just at that moment Benjamin came out of his tent, and his mother said, "A fine thing this is, you really do make work for me." "Then you all go to sleep in the sun."

Benjamin looked at his father, then he laughed because he looked so funny, all arms and legs and an upside down deckchair. "I suppose you think it's very funny Benjamin, but someone has to clear all this up" said his mother, trying not to smile.

Soon everything was ready and the whole mouse family was enjoying a lovely picnic.

It was now that Benjamin had a really good idea. "As all these things are in the garden, can we have a picnic?" he asked. Benjamin's father thought that this was a splendid idea, so he put up the deckchair for mother mouse to sit in. Then he made tea, whilst Benjamin and his sisters put the tablecloth on the little table and arranged the chairs around. Soon everything was ready, and the whole mouse family were enjoying a lovely picnic.

They all said what a clever little mouse Benjamin was to think of the picnic, and Father mouse was rather pleased because he wouldn't have to mow the lawn until tomorrow . . . . . .

. . . doing last minute things like putting Benjamin's toys away.

Benjamin's Kite

One fine day little Benjamin heard his mother say to father mouse that granny was coming that day to visit them. Now Benjamin, being the youngest mouse in the family, always liked old granny mouse's visits because she made a fuss of him and made him feel quite important. Benjamins two sisters did not look forward to granny's visits because they were older and were expected to behave like "grown-up mice," which they definitely were not, (although mother mouse really thought they were).

Before granny arrived there was much excitement and rushing about. Or rather Benjamin was excited and his mother and sisters were rushing about tidying the mouse house, and doing "last minute" things like putting Benjamins toys away, so it would take him days and days to find them again, much to his annoyance.

. . . *and a lovely kite for Benjamin.*

Finally granny arrived and Benjamin asked her if she had a present for him. His mother cuffed him behind the ear and said he was not to be so rude — which Benjamin could not understand — because granny always brought little presents.

Sure enough, granny had brought some presents. A fruitcake, two wicker baskets for his sisters and a lovely kite for Benjamin. Benjamin was very pleased with his kite, his sisters were a little envious (because not yet being "grown-up", they still liked playing with kites).

. . . he saw his granny sitting on her own in a rocking chair under the shade of an old apple tree.

Soon mother told her children to go out and play so that she could talk to granny mouse. However, Benjamin's sisters wanted to fly the kite, and were very nice to him. So he let them go with him along the path at the back of the mouse house, to a meadow which was just right for kite flying.

After a little while Benjamin got tired of this, partly because there was not very much wind, and partly because it seemed to him they wouldn't let him have a good turn at flying his kite. Soon he got tired of asking them to let him hold the string, so he walked back to the garden in a sulk.

When he walked in through the back garden gate he saw his granny sitting on her own in a rocking chair under the shade of an old apple tree. She had a rug over her knees, and a shawl over her shoulders.

*. . . so granny picked up the two sisters baskets, and
they walked down to the bottom of the garden . . .*

"What are you looking so glum for?" said granny. "My sisters won't let me play with my kite," replied Benjamin, kicking the gravel on the path. "Never mind, they will soon get tired of it, then you will have it to yourself." "Why don't we go and look for blackberries, and I'll tell you a little story," she continued. Benjamin brightened up at this because granny's stories were usually about when she was a young and rather mischievious little mouse — so granny picked up the two sisters baskets, and they walked down to the bottom of the garden where the blackberry bushes grew.

After a little while Benjamin was very happy. His granny was making him laugh with her stories, he was eating almost as many blackberries as he was putting in his basket, (which he was not supposed to do) and he was getting himself covered in blackberry juice. But he was enjoying himself, and so was granny — who loved to pick blackberries, almost as much as she loved telling Benjamin stories.

. . . and mother mouse was laying the table.

All too soon Benjamins sisters came along and said that mother was waiting, and tea was ready. (They had tired of kite flying soon after Benjamin left them). They scolded him for using their baskets — but granny said that it was only fair — after all, they had flown his kite.

When they all arrived for tea, father mouse was busy in the kitchen, and mother mouse was laying the table. "What ever have you been up to Benjamin!" she exclaimed. But granny came to his rescue and said it was her idea to pick blackberries.

So Benjamin was saved from a jolly good telling off, and also he could have something to look forward to, because you see granny would make some bramble jelly with the blackberries, and Benjamin really loved bramble jelly.

*. . . His mother and sisters were in the kitchen baking
a birthday cake . .*
. . . so Benjamin walked round the garden

Benjamin's Birthday

Tomorrow would be Sunday, and Sunday was also Benjamin's Birthday. But today he was at a loss to know what to do. His mother and sisters were in the kitchen baking a birthday cake (which he was not supposed to know about — as it was to be a surprise) so Benjamin walked round the garden with two pieces of wood throwing them up in the air and catching them.

He liked throwing and catching things. His mother always said "If you drop a cup, Benji can catch it before it breaks on the floor." But Benjamin was just waiting for tomorrow, when it would be his birthday.

. . . *he heard his father playing the piano, so Benjamin sat on the step and listened.*

Benjamin was looking for a stick he had dropped, when he heard his father playing the piano. It was not often he heard his father playing the piano, because all week he was at school, but on Saturday, sometimes his father played the piano, so Benjamin sat down on the step and listened. Benjamin loved to hear his father play, just as much as he disliked listening to his sisters practicing their scales. He wished he could play the piano as beautifully as his father.

Very soon his mother called him in for his tea, and before he knew, it was bed time. He went to bed quickly, because he wanted to wake up and unwrap his birthday presents.

. . . but kept dropping one or other of the clubs — and even banged himself on the head . . .

After breakfast he couldn't wait to open his presents. There was a new toy from his mother; two books from his sisters, and three juggling clubs (just the right size for him) which his father had made out of the legs of an old stool. After breakfast, Benjamin thanked everybody for their presents, and as it was a sunny day, went out into the garden, because he wanted to play at juggling.

He tried over and over again — but kept dropping one or other of the clubs — and even banged himself on the head. But Benjamin was not a mouse to give up easily, and by the afternoon he could throw his clubs in the air, one after the other, and catch them just like a clown in the circus.

. . . *whilst the mice ran round and round for musical chairs.*

That evening was to be special, because it was Benjamin's Birthday party. All his friends were invited. There were lots of nice things to eat and a Birthday cake (which was supposed to be a surprise — but Benjamin did not tell anybody that his mother and sisters had made it).

After the mice had eaten, they all played games. Benjamin's father played the piano, whilst the mice ran round and round for musical chairs.

After that he played again for "pass the parcel." Benjamin was very proud of his father. He was especially pleased when he won the prize in the middle of the parcel. Some of his friends said what a clever dad he had to play the piano so well, and Benjamin wished he could play — but his little paws went every which way when he tried to play, much to his disappointment.

And now Benjamin will perform . . .

Just then his father said that he thought it was time for everyone to do their party tricks. So they joined in to tell stories or sing songs and little harvest mouse picked nuts out of the air (which everyone loved — because they thought it was magic). But some mice didn't have anything at all they could do. Lastly it was Benjamin's turn, and he could not think of anything at all. Everyone was saying "Come on Benji give us a party trick" and he was getting just a little embarrassed, when his mother whispered in his ear "Why don't you show them your juggling?— I was watching you in the garden this morning, you are very good you know." At this little Benjamin's eyes brightened up, so he ran to his bedroom to fetch his new clubs. As he came back his father said, "And now Benjamin will perform a juggling trick." All the mice sat round, and Benjamin stood in the middle with his new clubs and started to throw them up into the air — one after the other. He really was quite clever, the mice cheered and clapped. Benjamin felt very proud, and all his friends said it was the best party trick of all.

The early morning sun shone brightly on the wall opposite the bed where Benjamin slept.

Benjamin's Castle

The early morning sun shone brightly on the wall opposite the bed where Benjamin slept. There was a soft swishing noise, like someone sweeping a path with a big hard broom, only a long way off. It was this soft noise which woke Benji up.

He opened his eyes, shut them quickly and rubbed them with his little paws. Then he opened them again. There on the wall were four little squares of bright sunlight. They should not be there he thought, then he remembered that he was not in his own room. Instead he was at a house by the sea.

This was the reason the sun shone onto the wall of his bedroom. He jumped out of bed, went skippity skip to the window and looked out. Then he gave a squeal of delight as, between the roofs of the houses on the other side of the lane he saw a small patch of dark blue. That, he thought, is the sea.

. . . so he picked up his bucket and spade, walked a
little way to where the sand was still wet and started
to dig.

Benjamin did not want to eat any breakfast that morning. But his Mother said "No breakfast — no beach today," so Benjamin ate his breakfast. Then, he had to wait for hours, (so it seemed) until everything was ready for their trip to the sea-side Benjamin ran ahead followed by his two sisters, then his Mother and Father who were carrying the big picnic basket.

Very soon he became tired of paddling at the waters edge, (because mice are not very fond of swimming), so he picked up his bucket and spade, walked a little way to where the sand was still wet and started to dig.

After a while Benji's sisters came to help him, but he was a little annoyed because they didn't understand how he was trying to make a moat for his sandcastle. Then he had an idea, "Why don't you go and collect some seaweed to make flags for the sandcastle?" he said, so they went off to find seaweed and left Benji to finish his castle.

. . . and said it was the finest sandcastle he had ever seen. This made Benjamin very proud indeed . . .

When he had finished it he stood back to admire his handiwork, unfortunately he stepped backwards right onto his Mother's paw, she jumped and Benjamin fell over, right into the moat (which was now full of water), but his Father quickly picked him up by the scruff of his neck, and putting him gently down said it was the finest sandcastle he had ever seen. This made Benjamin very proud indeed.

Just then his sisters came back with some seaweed and also some pebbles. So he placed the pebbles on the castle to look like windows, whilst his sisters made tiny flags out of the seaweed. Everyone agreed that this finishing touch made Benjamin's castle even more beautiful.

After they had walked all round it, admiring the moat, the drawbridge, the turrets and battlements and, of course, the flags and windows, Benji's Mother said she thought that it was time to all enjoy a picnic.

. . . *So he laid his head on his mother's lap and soon he
was fast asleep.*

They walked back up the beach, into some sand-dunes to where the picnic basket was. First the brightly coloured blanket was laid on the soft sand. Then out of the wicker basket came lots of nice things to eat and drink.

When the picnic was over and hardly anything was left at all, Benjamin felt a little sleepy, so he laid his head on his Mother's lap and soon he was fast asleep.

The sun moved slowly round, and a shadow cast by the tall grasses on the top of the sand-dune fell across Benjamin's face. This woke him up, and suddenly he remembered his sandcastle. He quickly ran off, shouting over his shoulder "I'm going to see my sandcastle."

... He was sitting down in a few inches of water his face was buried in his paws and he was crying.

When a few minutes had passed, his Mother decided to go and look for him, because she never let him out of sight on the beach. She walked slowly down the beach in the direction of the sandcastle, and soon saw Benjamin was sitting down in a few inches of water, his face was buried in his paws, and he was crying. In front of him, just a little way away, was a small hump of wet sand. Floating round about, gently washing to and fro were some small pieces of seaweed.

This was all that remained of Benjamin's magnificent sandcastle. Mrs Mouse sat down quietly beside him, put a paw on his shoulder and said "Didn't you know the tide would come in and cover your castle?" "No" he sobbed. "Well" she continued softly, "The tide has to come in and out to keep the beach clean. "But why does it have to knock down my lovely castle?" he said, trying hard to wipe away the tears running down his face.

So they walked back to meet his Father and sisters.

His Mother took out a handkerchief (which she always had with her), and gently wiped his eyes and cheeks. Then she gave it to him and said "Now blow your nose" in that tone of voice which always made him laugh.

"But why does the tide have to ruin my castle?" he said again. His Mother thought a minute before replying, then she said "If the tide never knocked down sandcastles, just think what would happen, in a short while the beach would be covered with them; we wouldn't be able to see the sea for sandcastles, and you would have no room to make one tomorrow." The thought of all the beach covered in sandcastles made Benjamin laugh so much he forgot he had been crying.

"I think we should all go back to our holiday home and have a nice hot dinner, don't you?" said his Mother. So they walked back to meet his Father and sisters. Benjamin was glad his sisters had not seen him crying, and he was really happy because tomorrow he could make another sandcastle.

... *jumped out of bed and ran to open the curtains*

The Happy Dream

Winter had been around for a long time and Benjamin was fed up with it.

Then, one morning, he woke up to see his bedroom looking very, very bright. Quickly he jumped out of bed and ran to open the curtains. What he saw made him jump up and down and clap his little paws with excitement. For during the night it had snowed, and as far as his eyes could see, everything was covered with soft, white snow.

... favourite wintertime breakfast of porridge with honey

The first thing he wanted to do was to run and play outside, but Mrs Mouse caught him as he ran into the kitchen, and said that before he went out, he should eat his breakfast, (which was Benjamins favourite wintertime breakfast of porridge with honey).

Soon Benjamin was out in the garden running around . . .

Soon Benjamin was out in the garden, running around looking at how everything had changed, and discovering all sorts of things hidden under the snow. He would have liked to have played with his sisters, but they did not want to go out into the cold.

Then he remembered his friend, the tiny harvest mouse, so he ran through the snow, all the way to the big field at the end of the apple orchard.

Benjamin walked slowly round the edge of the field calling to his tiny friend . . .

It was a long time since he had seen his friend the harvest mouse, and as he ran, Benjamin thought about all the games that they would play in the snow.

When Benjamin reached the edge of the field, it looked very strange indeed. The field looked as if it had no end, and poking up through the wide flat carpet of snow were countless stalks, like withered brown drinking straws.

Benjamin walked slowly round the edge of the field, calling to his tiny friend, but no answer came. "I wonder what has become of harvest mouse?" he thought to himself.

. . . walked away sadly.

The sun went behind a cloud, making the snow look rather grey. By now Benjamin was extremely cold, also a little tired. Benjamin called Harvest mouse one last time, but there was only a sigh as the wind started to blow flurries of snow across the field, so Benjamin turned round and walked sadly away.

. . . curled up in front of the fire and soon was fast asleep.

When he finally reached home, there was a lovely warm fire and a beautiful smell of something good cooking for dinner.

After Benjamin had eaten as much as his little tummy could hold, he curled up on the rug in front of the fire, and was soon fast asleep.

There was his friend, the tiny Harvest mouse.

As the fire gently warmed his back, Benjamin had a lovely dream. He dreamt that it was summertime. The sun shone from a bright blue sky, small cotton wool clouds followed their shadows across the cornfield, birds were singing, butterflies opened their powder-painted wings, and grasshoppers chattered to one another. And there, at the edge of the cornfield something caught his eye, right at the top of a long, slender cornstalk. As Benjamin went closer, his little heart raced with happiness. For there was his friend, the tiny harvest mouse.

On the way down the stairs he bumped into his father.

The Little Tree

Frost had made the dead leaves crisp and coated the grass with silver, which made it sparkle like magic in the early morning sun. Benjamin wanted to go out and play, but his mother was not so sure.

"It's very cold outside Benjamin" she said in a can't-you-do-something-else tone of voice.

Benjamin went to his room, but it was rather untidy — and he didn't really feel like cleaning it up. So he wandered off to find his sisters.

On his way down the stairs, he bumped into his father. "Whats the matter with you little fellow?" he said kindly. "Can't you think of anything to do on a lovely fine morning like this?" "Well — no" replied Benjamin, hoping his father wouldn't find him some arduous job — like clearing up his room.

So he wandered off to find his sisters.

"Let me see" said father mouse to himself, "I know, why don't you go for a brisk walk and get some fresh air? You could collect some dry twigs for me to light the fire with." Benjamin thought about this. It seemed quite a good idea. His father thought about it too. Then he added "You can go with your sisters. It will do you all good to get out." But secretly he also knew that the sisters would bring Benjamin home before his little paws got too cold.

Benjamin and his sisters were playing a super game of hide and seek.

So it was that Benjamin and his sisters were playing a super game of hide and seek, (having forgotten all about the firewood.) Benjamin went to hide under his favourite little evergreen tree which grew at the corner of the meadow, but when he got there the little tree was nowhere to be seen.

He looked all around in vain, then he noticed a small stump, poking up through the pine needles.

Benjamin just could not understand. Big trees sometimes got blown down in a strong wind, but this was only a small tree. And now it had gone!

Very soon, Benjamin's sisters found him, (mainly because he wasn't hiding). They too were puzzled by the disappearance of the little tree.

"Perhaps it got eaten," one of them said. "Or maybe it has been blown away" said the other — helpfully. But when they saw the trunk cut off cleanly, they had to agree that both ideas were extremely unlikely.

Then he noticed a small stump poking up through the pine needles.

As they were looking at where the tree had been, Benjamin gave a little shiver. His sisters agreed that the best thing they could do was to go home, (for they were all beginning to feel rather cold) and see if mother or father mouse could explain what had happened to the tree.

When they arrived home, hot and breathless from racing each other, mother and father mouse could not make head nor tail of what they were saying, because they all talked at once. "Just a moment you three" said father mouse, holding up a paw for silence. "Come in and warm yourselves by the fire and tell me what the problem is."

Benjamin's sisters looked at him, because it was he who had discovered the little tree stump. So he told his father all about it.

When he had finished his story, father mouse nodded, then he looked into the fire, gave it a poke to stir up some flames, and thought about the missing tree.

... *He took a deep breath, settled himself in his chair,
and this is what he told them.*

The three young mice sat patiently looking, first at the fire — then at their father. After a little while he took a deep breath, settled himself into his chair, and this is what he told them.

"Some families" he said "are not so fortunate as us mice. They live a long way from each other, so they only get together perhaps once a year. When that once-a-year time comes, they all give each other presents and have lots of nice food to eat. They decorate their homes in bright colours. They play games and tell stories and all sorts of other things as well.

So I'm told — sometimes they also have a little tree, which they cover with decorations and even small things to eat, because its a special occasion for them."

At this point father mouse paused. "Most probably, your little tree is in some home, with decorations on it and family presents spread underneath."

. . . lots of happy days together.

"Now I must go and see what your mother is up to" he said, and left the three little mice by the fire. They sat for a while, thinking about what their father had told them. Finally Benjamin spoke. "I think we are really lucky to not have to wait for this once-a-year time, don't you? We have lots of happy days together, and little surprise presents every now and again.

For once his sisters agreed with him, and they were not sad anymore about the little tree.

"There are many more stories of Benjamin for you to read. In Book 2, Benjamin meets a very special friend — a white mouse . . ."